IN PRAISE OF
THE MIND HACK RECIPE

"Jason has a unique way of teaching this work, he has taken away all the fluff, and just left the information that is needed. His mix of giving techniques in an easy to understand manner, are backed up by inspirational videos that back up his theory and quantify it."

Steve Bullock

"Hey Jason! Just wanted to write you to let you know how much I love the book! It's amazing to see not only manifestation techniques are taught in it, but also things like Qigong and many other interesting topics. Even for someone talking Dutch it was very clear and easy to read. I loved it, this is powerful! Thank you so much."

Evie Hallo

"Jason, wanted to let you know, the new book is terrific! It has some ideas from the Uberman book, which I also enjoyed but this one has some new and inspirational ideas that I am eager to try! Plus, it's a good reference book to keep close. Keep up the great things you are doing! Great material!"

Terri Schiavone

"Thank you for sharing all you have over the years in helping others including myself in finding joy and abundance! You are GOLD Jason Mangrum. Following your journey for the past 10 or so years has been fun and enlightening!"

Sheryl Delaplane

"Wow... Such beautiful and pretty interesting title. I am gonna keep my other books aside and read this one first... I would love to get my brain hacked. Thanks Jason for introducing such extraordinary and creative work... Truly inspirational, beneficial and appreciable!"

Jyosana Gupta

"Thanks for the book. What I have read so far is pure gold. The relaxation technique really works. Next I'm going to get onto the money manifestation!"

Marjorie Thorton

7 Proven Techniques to Hack Your Brain
for Amazing Mind Powers

THE MIND
HACK RECIPE

JASON MANGRUM

NEW YORK

NASHVILLE • MELBOURNE • VANCOUVER

THE MIND HACK RECIPE

© 2018 Jason Mangrum

Published in New York, New York, by Morgan James Publishing. Morgan James is a trademark of Morgan James, LLC.
www.MorganJamesPublishing.com

The Morgan James Speakers Group can bring authors to your live event. For more information or to book an event visit The Morgan James Speakers Group at www.TheMorganJamesSpeakersGroup.com.

MEDICAL DISCLAIMER: This book is not intended to be a substitute for the services of health care professionals. Neither the publisher nor the author is responsible for any consequences incurred by those employing the remedies or treatments reported herein. Any application of the material set forth in the following pages is at the reader's discretion and is his or her sole responsibility.

ISBN 978-1-68350-252-4 paperback
ISBN 978-1-68350-253-1 eBook
Library of Congress Control Number:
2016915820

Front Cover Design:
John Weber

Cover Wrap & Interior Design:
Megan Whitney
Creative Ninja Designs
megan@creativeninjadesigns.com

In an effort to support local communities, raise awareness and funds, Morgan James Publishing donates a percentage of all book sales for the life of each book to Habitat for Humanity Peninsula and Greater Williamsburg.

Get involved today! Visit
www.MorganJamesBuilds.com

CONTENTS

FOREWORD
DR. JOE VITALE

Mind Powers...

Extra-sensory perception...

Instant "miracle" healings...

Are these merely products of a wild and wanting imagination... are they a fluke—or is there something else going on?

Well, it depends on who you're asking.

Some people can see a real miracle happen right in front of them, and they still won't believe it's possible.

Others can see, hear and feel the miraculous in everyday life.

And yet, there are those who are somewhere in the middle, investing most of their time and intention into manifesting these miracles.

The truth is, everyone's method is different.

Some methods do work better than others.

Almost every method out there comes with its own set of rules and regulations, beliefs and philosophies.

These can take years to learn… and lifetimes to master.

Who's got that kind of time to waste?

Not me.

And you probably don't, either.

That's why I love this book.

It's more like a recipe book for mind power and miracles.

Let me explain.

If you want to make a delicious home-cooked meal, you don't need to learn the entire history of the food industry...

Or, the personal beliefs of the chef who wrote down the recipe.

It doesn't matter what those beliefs are.

If you follow every step of the recipe, you get a delicious meal.

In a similar way, you can unlock mental abilities and manifest miracles in your life, simply by following the recipes inside this little book.

Belief is not needed to experience these results.

There's no history lesson on these techniques, or why they work.

You don't need to study or practice for months or years to use them.

Jason has boiled these techniques down to "just the meat" in a series of steps you can perform just about anywhere to notice real changes.

xw What can these techniques do?

Imagine you could...

- Flip an instant switch for creativity "on demand"

- Push a button on your wrist and stress melts away...

- Access your intuitive abilities anytime you want

- Tap into your natural healing powers

- Supercharge your manifesting ability for money (or anything else)

- "See" in real-time how close you are to manifesting your goal

- Extract information directly from the subconscious mind

- And too much more to list here...

These techniques are just "training wheels."

They're designed to give your conscious mind something to do, so that it believes it's doing something.

The real work is done by the subconscious, which has access to much greater amounts of data than our conscious minds could ever imagine.

But "doing nothing" makes no sense to the conscious mind. So instead of fighting it, you can give it what it craves...

A set of rituals. A series of steps. An action plan to follow.

This often helps people achieve their goals faster and easier.

Once you've used the techniques enough to experience the results you're looking for, you don't need to use them anymore.

When you've installed these programs in your mind and reinforced them through repetition, and they have been validated by seeing positive results, then you no longer need to use the techniques.

So practice these, until you don't need them.

I've known Jason Mangrum for more than a decade, and he has a gift for cutting out the useless garbage and slicing right to the heart.

When I told him I wanted to sell more books, he figured out a way to sell $50 million dollars' worth of them in one fell swoop on eBay.

The publicity alone was worth millions.

When I told him I wanted a piece of software that had the same effect of reading my Attractor Factor book, he took just the 5 steps taught in the book and made an amazing piece of online software using nothing but a few lines of code on a single web page.

Sales for the book soared.

I once hired him to create a marketing campaign for me, and the results made my eyes pop out of my head… over 30,000 visitors came rushing to my web site in one day.

Orders were flying off the shelves.

Jason's ability to manifest the impossible is awe-inspiring.

His gift for the miraculous is undeniable.

And his techniques can unlock gifts within you, too.

Just remember, when you master the technique… discard it.

As if you're removing the training wheels.

How will you know when you're ready?

You can do the technique without thinking about it. It becomes a force of habit. And you begin to see miracles happen in your life.

Things can manifest that have no logical explanation.

Eventually, your conscious mind will have no choice but to give in, realizing that it doesn't know as much as it thought.

And that's when miracles can occur without your intention.

They're not even miracles to you anymore. A miracle is something that rarely happens.

Otherwise it's just natural. It just happens.

So read this book, follow the techniques and enjoy your miracles.

Ao Akua,

Dr. Joe Vitale

#1 Bestselling Author of *Attractor Factor* and *Zero Limits*
Star of the hit movie *"The Secret"*
www.MrFire.com

WELCOME TO THE WORLD OF MIND HACKING

My name is Jason Mangrum.

I'm an author, a consultant for business and personal development, a marketing strategist, copywriter, piano player, mind warrior, consciousness explorer, innovator and visionary.

I've also learned some key secrets about the awesome power of consciousness and how to "tweak" it to achieve some truly astonishing effects in the physical, mental and emotional realms of being.

I will be your insider guide to the once highly secretive, often misunderstood and vastly underestimated science of hacking the mind.

Within these pages, you'll learn 7 mental and energetic techniques to:

- Magnetically begin to attract better finances and new opportunities for growth

- Relieve your stress-response in practically any situation

- Learn how to manifest your desires with "bulls-eye" accuracy

- Actually feel "chi" flowing through the air and your body in 3 minutes or less

- An ancient Taoist secret for near-instant pain relief in just 20 minutes a day

- A revolutionary new tool for attracting success effortlessly by watching movies

- And much, much more…

I'm extremely interested in your results!

There's no "magic" in this book.

Although, it might seem like it is magic when you see results.

Your mind is far more powerful than you can imagine.

Ancient teachers, masters of meditation and energy practitioners from all over the world, in every different culture, have their own closely-guarded secrets.

The alchemists, magicians and sorcerers of the past have become the chemists, scientists and hypnotists of today.

What was once seen and believed to be "supernatural" has achieved a much greater psychological understanding, and has given access to mental abilities that were once considered "sorcery" or magic.

These techniques have either been uncovered and practiced along my personal journey of self-discovery, or developed by myself as a result of fusing several mystical traditions and practices together.

I hope you enjoy this "recipe book" of pure empowerment, and apply these techniques to enhance every aspect of your entire life.

Within this book, you have some real tools on the table that have proven to be effective at unlocking abilities and potentials you never thought you had before… use them wisely and share your results with others!

Live in Magnificence,

Jason Mangrum

Author

www.personaldevelopmentwithjason.com/blog

1

MIND HACK

The Instant "Stress Relief" Button

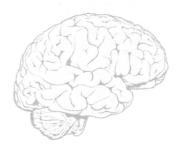

Are you easily stressed?
Do you find it hard to stay focused?

Isn't it frustrating when that terrible anxiety kicks in and you feel overwhelmed at your situation and hopeless to change it?

It's no secret that stress is a killer... it shortens our lifespan, creates numerous health issues both mental and physical... eradicates our sense of confidence and self-worth... promotes procrastination and fear of failure, which leads to stagnation (feeling "stuck") and much more.

Stress is a deadly disease of the mind, which affects us physiologically.

Wouldn't it be amazing if you could literally stop stress dead in its tracks, and even reverse the effects of it in your body and mind?

Now what if you could do this in as little as 60 seconds?

Thanks to the HeartMath™ Institute, now you can.

They've developed a scientific process called the "Quick Coherence Technique" that allows you to easily access a state of mind/body coherence in about 60 seconds by releasing stress and stopping emotions such as frustration, irritation, anxiety and anger.

According to their web site, this helps you:

- Reduce stress right in the moment.
- Feel positive, focused, calm and energized.
- Perform at your best.
- Access creativity, intuition and higher-level decision making.

You can read the instructions or listen to an audio recording, guiding you through each step of the "Quick Coherence Technique" given away freely on their web site.

https://www.heartmath.org/resources/
heartmath-tools/quick-coherence-technique-for-adults/

Now here's where you can take this a step further…

Once you've done the technique a few times and are familiar with it, each time you sense yourself within the "coherent" state, gently press into a spot on your wrist (either one) and hold it there, while you're still feeling yourself being aware of the sensations of coherence.

Make sure each time you practice The Quick Coherence Technique, you press the exact same spot, on the same side, in the same way, while you are experiencing the coherent state.

After doing this repetitiously for approximately 7-10 days, you will begin to notice that simply by "pressing the button" those feelings and sensations you have experi-

enced within the coherent state will rush back to you—
without repeating the full technique.

You can think of this as installing a hypnotic trigger
mechanism.

Through simple repetition, you can "assign" any sensation, memory or feeling to any physical touch… so that
when the same area is pressed, the subconscious program
for creating coherence is activated.

With practice, this becomes your instant "stress relief" button!

You can also access the coherent state to switch on
your natural intuitive abilities to connect with deeper
parts of yourself for exploring consciousness, deep meditation, self-healing and much more.

MIND HACK

A Technique for Feeling "Chi" in 3 Minutes

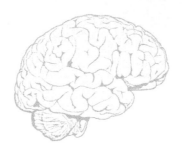

You've most likely heard stories of Zen masters and Shaolin monks performing incredible feats of super-human strength and stamina...

Or, maybe you heard about the medicine-less hospital in China where Qigong practitioners visibly dissolved a cancerous tumor in their patient within about 3 minutes, using no medicine.

And if you do some real research, you'll find the success rates of these practices is far beyond anything the western-rational mind can grasp.

There are thousands of documented case-studies of patients with "incurable" diseases, health issues, mental problems, pains and other ailments who have been miraculously "cured" by these methods.

And if that's not enough to convince you, watch this video of a chi Master who can harness and project his chi to put animals to sleep, from a distance!

https://www.youtube.com/watch?v=GNuPJEiEo5o

But how is it possible?

No matter if you're searching for the answer in the mountains of Tibet, the temples of China or seeking out the great Huna sorcerers of Hawaii, you'll discover a "life force energy" that is present within all things, is intelligent, is attracted and directed by intention and focused awareness, imbues the user with seemingly "mystical" powers of healing and protection from harm for self and others, and is believed to exist beyond time and space.

In the eastern tradition, this is called chi, qi or ki.

And while it isn't recognized by the western scientific community due to our inability to track, measure and validate it using conventional technology, some have figured out a way to measure its effects using a "subtle energy detector."

Dr. William Tiller is a pioneer of Psycho-energetic Science, who has devised such a device to track and measure the effects of directed intention in a few astonishing ways... which has now been replicated in ten different laboratories in the U.S. and Europe.

These are:

1.   To increase the pH of water in equilibrium with air by +1 PH units and with no intentional chemical additions;

2.   To decrease the pH of the same type of water in equilibrium with air by -1 pH units and with no intentional chemical additions;

3.   To significantly increase the in vitro thermodynamic activity of the liver enzyme alkaline phosphatase (ALP) via a 30-minute exposure to an intention-host device "conditioned" space and;

4. To significantly increase the in vitro ATP/ADP ratio in the cells of living fruit fly larvae via lifetime exposure (~28 days) to an intention-host device "conditioned" space so that they would become more physically fit and thus exhibit a significantly reduced larval development time, to the adult fly stage.

The results of Dr. Tiller's experiments have been staggering.

To read his full white paper on "An Experimental Investigation of Some Reconnective-Healing Workshops via a Unique Subtle Energy Detector" you can access the direct download PDF here:

http://www.tillerinstitute.com/pdf/
White%20Paper%20XI.pdf

To learn more information about Dr. Tiller's research and gain free access to his documented experiments and peer-reviewed studies, visit his official web site at:

http://www.tillerinstitute.com/

Now that you're aware of the more practical applications of "chi" through breathing, movement, focus and directed intention, here's how you can activate it, feel it, "see" it and begin moving it around in about 3 minutes or less (with some practice.)

Foo Tiock Feng is a master Qigong practitioner who gives information and actual techniques for harnessing and projecting chi, and even creating a "real, colorful Qi ball" using only your hands and chi energy.

You can read his material for harnessing and emitting chi on his blog at:

http://tffoo.blogspot.com/2012/07/
qi-gong-introduction-to-qi-emission-qi.html

According to Mr. Feng, you must first build up the chi energy before you are able to actually construct the Qi ball. He advises to practice cultivating chi for at least one hour per day.

Harnessing, activating and cultivating chi/qi/ki is literally one of the greatest secrets available for obtaining "superhuman" abilities.

MIND
HACK

Ten Steps
to Hack
Your Brain

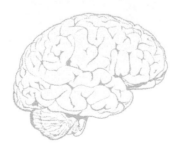

Before Hacking Your Mind—You Must Understand This!

Just as a computer "hacker" must first learn how a computer works from the inside-out, so too you must learn how your mind works, if you hope to manipulate it to create lasting change for you.

Your mind can either assist you in your goals, or keep you from them.

The mind and memory are inextricably connected.

For example, when you think of something you want, your mind fires back at you with every conceivable reason or excuse why you can't.

These ideas are taken from memories associated with why you can't have the thing you want, and "logical" or reasonable excuses why it just isn't realistic for you to possess that which you desire.

These ideas of course also come with feelings attached to them which compound the problem and make you feel like your desire is an impossibility in the moment.

And it gets worse from there!

These feelings change your whole attitude about what you can do.

They also affect your motivation, drive and enthusiasm for action.

These emotions can make you feel helpless, useless and out of control.

Beyond hope. Lost. At the end of your rope.

Now keep in mind, this is how your mind and emotions rob you of success in accomplishing anything you want. No exceptions!

So what's the first step in getting your mind under your control?

You must first identify the root-cause, or the real problem.

And no matter who you are, what your background is, where you were born or grew up, how much money you have (or lost), how difficult your life was or is, the root-cause is NOT outside of you.

This is often the most difficult concept to come face-to-face with.

It seems to be interwoven into our society to want to blame others and point the finger in any direction but our own.

You can have two groups of people—group A comes from a difficult background and spends more time complaining about their misfortune than doing anything to change it.

Group B also comes from an unfortunate background, but reacts to it differently and develops a habitual system of doing something (even one thing) every single day to change their situation... guess who's going to get further ahead in life?

It isn't about what happened or happens to you...

100% of the time, it's about how you react to your circumstances and situations that determines the level of success in your life.

How you respond is determined by the perspective you choose to experience the situation from, the mental attitude you hold and the ability to remain emotionally neutral, so your emotions don't get the best of you.

This doesn't mean lying to yourself. When things are bad, they're bad.

If you try to cover up your reality with happy thoughts and "positive thinking" you're only lying to yourself (in your mind) and this makes you feel even worse.

That doesn't help!

What you need is to completely rewire your brain.

That way, what you "thought" you perceived, you begin to see differently, from a new, more expanded perspective.

Einstein once said, "A problem can never be solved from the same level of consciousness that created it." And he's right!

How you are seeing the problem now, is what is standing in your way.

It's robbing you of enthusiasm. It's causing you to shut off the myriad of opportunities to create something better for yourself.

As long as you are observing the issue as it is, it cannot change. But that's because you cannot change. Or you think you can't.

Rewrite the instruction code in your mind so that these excuses are replaced by empowering commands that inspire consistent action.

The real question then becomes... how much do you want change?

Are you willing to finally let go of how you have perceived the problem, issue or circumstance and entertain the idea, that just perhaps, you have been standing in your own way all this time?

There's only one real way to do that.

It's to form what is called a Subconscious Acting Habit.

The good news is this is an automatic process.

What if you committed yourself to doing ONE thing every day (no matter how large or small) that outright defies your limitations?

Let's say you have trouble being social in public for instance...

What do you think would happen if you suddenly threw yourself into a social situation and began introducing yourself to one new person every day, even though it might scare you to death?

Everything inside you will say "This is crazy! What are you doing? Why are you acting like this? This is NOT like you at all! Stop it!"

Then your thoughts will immediately pick up on this and will present you with memories and imaginings of you standing there, not knowing what to say or do next after opening your mouth...

That's not a situation you want to be in, so you shut down.

Then, imagine you see someone who looks a lot like you walk up to the person you were going to introduce yourself to, and start talking.

This person was standing right beside you, was given the exact same opportunity as you, but he/she sees the situation somehow differently, and therefore reacts in a completely different way.

The only real difference was the internal dialogue that played in his/her mind and the mental and emotional associations which inspired and motivated the person to take action.

So, to inspire a different action, you must feel different first. Your feelings can influence your thought patterns, and vice-versa.

It's much easier to influence your feelings than your thinking.

If you feel rotten on the inside, but try to bury the feeling with positive thoughts, you'll get nowhere!

But if you are feeling positive, energetic and inspired, it's much easier to align your thinking patterns with those feelings since that's the emotional state you are in. Then things begin "flowing" much easier.

So for this technique, I'm going to give you a mental exercise you can practice to FEEL better fast.

Once you can influence your feelings, you'll be in a much more beneficial space to manifest real change.

1. Standing up or sitting down, get comfortable and become aware of right now, the present moment.

2. Take a deep breath inward, let it out and at the same time feel your shoulders drop and feel the energy move downward.

---

3. Your awareness should now be centered on your belly. Hold your attention there and take another deep breath inward while holding that space. As you breathe in, feel that area expand as your lungs expand to take in the air.

4. As you breathe out, hold the space of awareness in your belly and feel the air pushing down into that area, causing your awareness to expand even further, outside the body.

5. Take a few more breaths, and imagine that as you are breathing in, you are connecting with the "chi" (life force) within the air itself, and are "breathing it" into your body. It's not enough to imagine it, you want to FEEL it as it's happening.

6. On the exhale, "push" this energy down into your belly and fill up that "space" you created and feel expanding with each breath...

7. After a few breaths, you should feel the space expanding and extending beyond the body. Even if you think you are only imagining it, go with it anyway and FEEL this happening.

8. You should begin to feel a new subtle energy—a new vibration within the space you created, even outside the body! While in this space, bring your attention to your problem. Notice how it somehow seems more "distant" than before. You're holding your thought of this problem, this lack, this limitation inside this space you created (called the Heart Field) and you can feel the difference in the intensity of the thought as it doesn't seem to carry as much weight as it did before...

9. Now that the "charge" is being neutralized from the thought within this powerful space of active consciousness, create a new thought that completely opposes the other thought. Feel what the energy of STRENGTH would feel like, and breathe it into that space, enveloping the now-weakened thought with its much more powerful successor.

10. Breathe in the new energy and entirely fill the space with it. Know in your heart that you are consciously breathing in a new opportunity to experience something different, and let that thought overtake you, filling you with peace and excitement of what the new opportunity might bring you.

From this new perspective, do you feel there might be some opportunities you may have been missing because you were stuck in the "tunnel vision" of your past limiting thoughts and feelings?

Do you now feel more open and receptive?

If you want to RECEIVE something, you must be receptive.

You must be in a receptive state.

Most people who are trying to receive something are often in a projective state, where they allow their thoughts and feelings to be "projected outward" against whatever information is coming in, which naturally repels the new information.

The technique above (regardless of theories of why/ how it works) is designed to change your perspective by altering your consciousness and placing you in a receptive

THE MIND HACK RECIPE

state—which causes the mind to look for new information and opportunities to match that state.

These ten steps can be performed easily in five minutes or less, especially once you practice the technique a few times.

Try this... do the simple technique above at least once per day, for the next 30 days. Mark it on your calendar if you have to... this is how to create real change, so it's important.

After 21-30 days of performing this technique, you'll develop a Subconscious Acting Habit, which begins building actual neural-pathways in the brain, hard-wiring the information.

It then becomes an automatic response to whatever problems or issues you are facing. The autopilot takes over (the subconscious) and the technique becomes an effortless reflex.

It literally just becomes a part of your normal operation.

You become much more aware of new opportunities in abundance to change whatever circumstance or situation you find yourself in, and have the mental and emotional

capacity to deal with things from a much calmer, more col-
lective perspective.

Plus, the excitement from "looking for what's different than before" causes you to become inspired more easily,
practically on command.

And once you're inspired, it's much easier to take action
on new opportunities that present themselves in this new
light of reality.

MIND HACK 4

Manifesting Money— A Quantum Thought Experiment

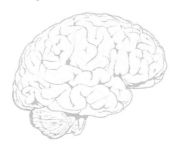

Let me ask you a question.

If you could, how many times would you turn a single dollar bill, into two one dollar bills?

Sounds like a pretty cool magic trick, doesn't it?

What if there was a way to figure this out? The logical mind is okay with having two bucks, so there's less subconscious resistance to manifesting that amount of money.

You can imagine it right now.

And from there, you can bring it into your experience.

Manifesting money, wealth and success, prosperity and abundance are physical manifestations brought into existence through a conduit which is created for, and aligned with that sole purpose.

The truth about manifesting anything is that thoughts appear and exist in your actual experience from the instant you create them, in the "mental realm" of your reality. So you do manifest instantly…

The "trick" is figuring out how to convert that thought substance into something physical, something tangible you can hold in your hands.

And so, to bring that intent from the mental realm into the physical plane of existence, a conduit must be created. A wormhole if you will… a channel or "bridge" from one dimension to another.

To be clear, if you want more income, you have to open a channel to receive it. The amount of money you make is equal to the size and quality of the channel you create for it.

If you want 9-5 type money, you get a 9-5 type job.

If you want to write your own paycheck, you own a business.

Those are two possible channels.

Both have their benefits and disadvantages.

With a job, you have more financial stability, but no freedom.

With a business, you have more freedom, capacity for growth and the potential to earn a lot more money, but no stability.

You could earn $100 one month, and then $10 the next month.

I've had months where I'd clear $60k and then the very next month would be $7-10k. A majorly huge difference! But you can't make that kind of money working at a dead-end job.

Remember, you are rewiring your mind to accept new ideas, new suggestions… new information to expand and accelerate your mental, emotional and physical capacity for greater wealth, more abundance and a bigger income.

And since we're dealing with such a material thing as money, if you really want more of it, you realize that you are going to have to do something different than you're doing now, to get a different result.

You must change your thought patterns in relation to money, and having more of it in your life.

You must also change your emotions related to money.

When you change your thoughts and emotional connections to money, you begin to see the whole concept of money differently.

You also begin to accept new ideas about making money, and lose old fears associated with losing money.

Thanks to the power of the internet, wherever you are in the world you can now earn money.

Don't defeat yourself by thinking you're going to get rich, drive fancy cars, pay all your debts, etc....

That kind of thinking permeates through the "make money" niches (MMO, IM, MLM) and infects the minds of those who need it most.

Instead of hoping to get rich quick, start with a dollar.

If you can make $1, you can turn it into $2...

And if you set up the channel properly, you'll soon have a self-funding money machine that turns $1 into $2 over, and over again.

It is possible, when you perceive the concept in a different way.

Which is why we're spending so much time doing the "prep work" because beliefs and emotions you are holding within you MUST be identified, cleared and replaced for this to work for you...

I'm going to share with you a very powerful technique that I wrote in my book Uberman, called "The Money Manifestor."

The primary design of this technique is to rewire your mental and emotional associations to money.

Then, through a new lens of perspective, you can literally manifest more of it, in increasing levels and frequency.

No matter if you think the technique will work or not, or whatever theories to support or deny it, just do it. And watch what happens.

Do you need more money in your life right now?

Could you use some extra cash to pay your bills?

Would you like to learn about a revolutionary new formula to bring more money into your life without having to pay a dime for it?

Use the Money Manifestor—a special technique for manifesting money into your life right now.

By now you're either skeptical, curious or both. That's perfectly okay.

I'm here to present to you a formula I discovered utilizing a process of magnetization and the principle of incremental improvement.

Using this technique, you're going to experience your innate ability to manifest money, whenever you want.

I've learned over the years the best way to help yourself is to help others. By developing this technique, I'm using it to master my own ability to manifest money and showing others how to do it too. By releasing this into the public I'm activating the Law of Abundance and strengthening this particular morphic field to work faster and better for everyone.

The Law of Abundance suggests that the world and even the fundamental nature of the entire Universe is pure, unlimited abundance.

When we realize this and shift our perspective to see amazing abundance in everything from countless stars in the sky to the endless blades of grass on Earth, we open our mind to the understanding that by nature, all things are overflowing with abundance.

It is only when our perspective focuses on lack of abundance that we begin to create beliefs of limitations, control, fear, jealousy and even hate. This has led to wars, street violence, poverty, theft, and the desire to have power over others.

There is in fact, more than enough.

Everyone is entitled to a life of abundance and prosperity by birthright.

Your beliefs and programming since your birth have caused this ability to lie dormant within you… yet it remains in your subconscious, patiently waiting to be reactivated.

This technique serves to activate your latent ability to manifest money.

You'll begin as an Initiate, simply meaning—you're being "initiated" into this new way of manifesting money into your life.

By the time you've become proficient at using the technique you'll be known as a v10 Master Money Manifestor.

Just like any muscle, your mental abilities get stronger with practice and exercise. Herein is a method of tracking your progress and a new way of thinking about money so that you attract it more easily into your life.

From this point onward, forget about the physical manifestation of money… the green stuff with dead presidents on it. Instead, for this exercise you will equate money to value.

The value of money is now equivalent to your level of ability to manifest it.

The levels of your ability are as follows:

$1.00 = v1
$10.00 = v2
$20.00 = v3
$50.00 = v4
$100.00 = v5
$150.00 = v6
$250.00 = v7
$500.00 = v8
$750.00 = v9
$1,000.00 = v10

Your status indicates how quickly you're able to manifest money:

Initiate = 30 days or more
Apprentice = 29-14 days
Adept = 13-7 days
Scholar = 6-2 days
Master = 1 day

You begin at $1 and as you train using the technique given below, your ability to manifest money in larger amounts will increase and the time it takes to bring the manifestation into your physical experience will get shorter.

Imagine when you attain the ability to manifest $1,000 or more in a single day!

Once you've hit this mark, you can manifest anything you want by simply practicing the technique and expanding your belief system, using the incredible accomplishment of a v10 Master Money Manifestor to overcome everything!

The "Money Manifestor" Technique:

1. Sit still. Breathe in slow and deep in even breaths. When you inhale, feel energy in the form of pure white light come in through the top of your head and go straight down into your abdomen, about 2 inches down from your bellybutton. On exhale, see clear air with specks of negative energy in the form of dark flakes exit from your mouth. Repeat this process

until the clear air you breathe out is as pure as the white light coming in.

2. Close your eyes and imagine receiving the amount of money you want to experience. Beginners always start with $1.00, because it is often the easiest to manifest quickly. After all, anyone reading this Mind Hack will have most likely manifested $1.00 in their lifetime and there are no strong objections or limiting beliefs about having $1.00.

3. Do not be concerned with how the money comes to you. This part is vital and will prove itself when manifesting larger amounts of money in shorter periods of time. However you choose to visualize or imagine money coming to you is perfectly fine, but remain completely unattached to how the money is manifested into your physical experience.

4. Answer this very important question… "What will having this amount of money give me that I don't have right now?" If it's $1.00, then you can honestly answer that manifesting

that amount will build a foundation for you to build your belief that you can manifest higher amounts over time. If it's larger, go within and think of what this amount of money represents to you.

Explode with emotion and exclaim your answer within your own inner-universe behind closed eyelids.

5. Think of yourself as a giant magnet. When you inhale, feel the energy you want to attract (i.e. the energy of money) being forcefully pulled to you. Create this sensation of "pulling" into your body.

   You can feel it.

   Visualize receiving your desired amount of money in whatever symbolic form your mind presents to you, and when you inhale, you're pulling this specific, directed energy into your being. On exhale, feel your body from the inside out; pulsate with magnetic force and energizing power.

6. Continue magnetizing your visualization until you instinctively feel a "click" or a sudden

recession in energy. This is how you can tell your magnetization is complete and you'll feel the desired thought-form is now closer to manifesting into your physical life.

7.   Repeat this process every single day until the desired amount of money is manifested into your physical experience. When that happens, make a note of how many days it took you to manifest this amount of money in a journal or notebook. Find what status and level you're at and record that as well. You are now a Money Manifestor!

8.   Use incremental improvement to increase your ability to manifest money. Start with v1 ($1.00) and move up the scale, all the way to a v10 ($1,000.00). Be open to any and all opportunities that present themselves to bring this money to you. You'll quickly begin to notice how many opportunities suddenly emerge to manifest your desires.

Do not try to "skip" levels, but instead make a commitment to accomplish each level in the shortest amount of time. Doing this daily will raise your level and build your status quickly.

Again, do not be concerned with how the money will come to you.

You could receive your $1.00 through your normal paycheck with your job, by finding it on a street corner, by realizing you had $1.00 you weren't aware of in your pocket, or in any other way.

What many closed-minded people call coincidence is actually the energy of synchronicity in motion.

Synchronicity is how your desires are made manifest.

It may seem like nothing more than "coincidence" at first that you wanted to manifest $1, $10, $20 or even $50 and then magically received it, however it will become much clearer to you over time, and as you strengthen your belief system to incorporate manifestation into your daily life that you will realize this method works.

When you've reached the level of a v10 Master Money Manifestor, you'll know beyond the shadow of a doubt that you create your reality and can manifest anything you want!

Remember, you must practice manifesting these amounts of money in order and once you've manifested all the way through a v10 level, focus your intent on increasing your status by reducing the amount of time it takes you to progress through each level.

Within a very short time, your energy field will contain a strong magnetic force that pulls energy directed by your intent to you easily and effortlessly.

You can then go onto manifesting much larger amounts and watch the opportunities show up to bring you money in any amount, whenever you choose. You are now a master of money manifesting!

So, that's the internal game...

Do the technique and you'll be surprised.

Manifesting money is a skill, and just like with any skill, you get stronger, faster, better with practice.

Now, let's create a proper channel in the physical world to receive more money.

To do that (and skip over all the BS, hype and false promises that often come with it) you're going to need two things:

---

1. An item of value
2. An audience who wants the value

The item can be a physical thing, or it can be digital.

Or it can be a service.

I'm not going into the basics of Internet Marketing or Making Money in this Mind Hack. When you have the proper channels open and the right perspective, making money gets a lot easier to understand.

And it's the understanding that makes all the difference.

These days, you don't even have to sell something to make money.

With CPA (Cost per Action) offers, you can earn money by getting people to enter in their zip code into a form and click a button.

And then, there's AdSense where you can get paid every time someone clicks on a link. All you do is generate traffic to a web site with updated quality content on it, and you can make money.

Internet Marketers like to make it seem so much harder than it actually is, *if* you're willing to roll up your sleeves and do the work.

The shocking thing is, most people have so many preconceived ideas, beliefs and limitations about money that they're not willing to put in this kind of work (and would rather flip burgers!) because they haven't yet been "convinced" it's possible to make more money.

So with the Money Manifestor Technique, we're clearing out those old beliefs and limitations and rewiring those associations.

Now, you need clear and focused action to open the channel.

One of the best methods I've ever used (and continue to use to this day—because it works) is…

---

1. Develop something of value (an article, a free report, a digital product, eBook, plugin or software.)

2. Offer the value upfront in exchange for an email address.

3. Locate complementary products to your topic of value and join their affiliate program.

4. Go to their "Promo Tools" page, and copy their prewritten emails to promote their product

5. Add them into your Autoresponder sequence and repeat

This process is much easier than you might think.

And it's repeatable.

Once you put in the effort to setup the system, you focus on Step One (providing the value) and the system spits out money for you, on complete autopilot.

Basically, you "feed" it value, and your system turns it into money.

If you have something to share with the world, write it down.

That is value.

Everyone has specialized knowledge or experience in something.

And if other people share that same interest, you can share your value with those like-minded people, and you can make money.

You don't have to sell your value to make money.

That's where most people get tripped up and slowed down.

They think they have to create some big product or service and it has to be just perfect, etc... this is simply not the case at all.

Before I wrote the book Uberman, I lived very comfortably for years from ONLY doing the same five steps I just shared with you.

Give away your value. That's what draws people in. That's what gets their attention. Give it away up front. Then find other entrepreneurs who are selling their value, and promote their offers as an affiliate.

For more information on affiliate marketing, you can check out my book entitled, *Super Affiliate Ninja Secrets*.

www.SuperAffiliateNinjaSecrets.com

After a while, you can create your own product to sell, but why slow yourself down... just get started NOW and make some money first!

If you don't have a list of subscribers, you need one.

And then, you need an Autoresponder sequence.

Your focus should be on giving away awesome free value in exchange for becoming a subscriber.

Subscribers = Money

The Autoresponder sequence is a series of emails set to go out automatically by themselves on a schedule that you specify.

Your Autoresponder sequence serves to introduce yourself and your value, to build a relationship through providing that value, and to sell products and services that enhance the life of your subscribers. If you can't write, outsource it to someone who can. Anything you cannot do yourself, can be outsourced.

See what I mean about demonstrating value?

That's the ticket.

That's where you want to come from-sincerity and originality. I've been doing this for a long time, and this still works like magic.

5

MIND HACK

The "Bow & Arrow" Technique for Manifesting

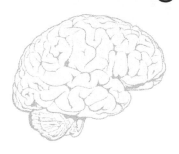

Using visualization and symbolism, you can communicate ideas to your subconscious mind that can unlock abilities beyond imagination.

You can also pull out information hidden deep within your subconscious that you may have never been consciously aware of.

While your conscious mind can process 7-10 bits of information per cycle per second of brainwave activity, the subconscious is capable of processing more than 40 billion bits of information per cycle.

That means there is WAY more information readily available to you, than you could even imagine possible.

Here's one unique way to leverage this innate ability...

It's called the "Bow & Arrow" Technique, and it allows you to practice increasing your accuracy of manifesting by giving you instant feedback responses direct from your subconscious, to you.

Here's the technique:

1. Imagine you're holding a bow and arrow. The bow represents your Will, your Intent. The arrow represents a thought-form you wish to manifest into physical reality.

2. See a target in the distance. An archer's circular target, with the red bulls-eye in the center. Notice a "100" on the red bulls-eye of the target. In the ring outside of the red bulls-eye, you see a 75. In the next ring, a 50. The next, a 25... and the outer-most ring of the target displays a 10. Everything else can be considered "missing the target" and thus a zero. The target represents the physical world. Your actual experience.

3. Now aim the arrow, knowing that it represents your thought-form. Your wish. Of course you want to aim for the red bulls-eye. The 100. As you pull back the arrow and feel the resistance, you realize the "pulling back" is an action of charging the arrow with force... which represents how you feel about, sense, taste, smell, hear and see your thought-form.

    Naturally, the more you pull back... the greater the force... the further, faster and stronger the arrow flies to its target, when you...

4. LET GO. Stop your thoughts. Free the bow-string and thus the arrow from your grip. Allow it to fly. It is now out of your control. It's in the air, headed for the target. All you did was aim, pull back and let go.

5. It is done. This next part is just for calibration. With a state of total non-attachment... "It's just an arrow"-take a few deep breaths... remain calm and relaxed... and casually observe the target.

Is the arrow there? Did it hit the bulls-eye, and get 100… or somewhere else resulting in a lower score? Did it miss the target completely?

Wherever you see the arrow, pay attention.

The number it lands on represents your subconscious or intuitive awareness of the weight of probability for that wish to manifest into the physical world.

If it's lower than 100, there's a reason why.

And it ALWAYS has to do with letting go.

Because, when you're reasoning, you're in left-brain land.

See, nothing actually happens (or can) until you truly let go.

You can hold onto that bow and arrow all day long… string pulled back as far as it'll go… but all that'll happen is you'll eventually tire yourself out and either give up-no longer pulling back, and hence, no force… or, you'll get out of your own way, and let go.

If you get anything less than 100, you need to adjust your AIM, or pull back a little further.

You have endless thoughts and so, you have endless arrows.

No limits.

You can use this tool as many times as you want… forever… just remember, if you get a 100, you don't need to use the tool again for the same thought-form.

It will manifest, so long as you stay out of the way.

And the very best way, to stay out of the way, is to move your awareness into your heart-field… which is actually an energetic bio-field surrounding the heart that reaches from the heart area, down through the pit of the stomach… within and around the bellybutton.

It's a big field!

Interestingly, when you really want to "get out of the way" drop down into this area.

Just become aware of the area.

That's it.

Just "whoosh" it right there.

Get out of your head, and into your heart... so you can get a "gut feeling" which is your access-point to the right-brain hemisphere, and the zero-point state of total coherence!

You access your left-brain when your awareness is in your head.

Here, you're limited to logic.

All the affirmations, visualizations, tips, tricks, tools and techniques in the world can't help you. Your grip on the hose is too tight-and your left-brain likes it that way, because that makes it feel safe. Secure. In control.

But drop into your heart-field, and notice what you feel.

You feel.

When you use what you learned from The Quick Coherence Technique from HeartMath, and at the same time drop your awareness into your heart space… magic happens.

You gain a deep sense of Self Awareness.

This combined with the Bow & Arrow Technique I gave you can be very powerful, on many levels. As with anything… the more you use it… the more you become aware of it… the easier it becomes.

The stronger it gets.

The quicker and clearer you'll see the effects of your cause.

This is the sole purpose of cultivation practice.

Enjoy your new-found abilities to make your wishes come true.

MIND HACK

Ancient Taoist Secret for Instant Pain Relief

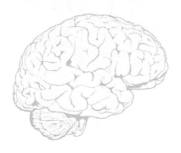

Before I begin describing this particular Mind Hack, I must inform you that I am not a doctor. The claims being made are not my claims, and I can neither support nor deny the efficacy of the information you're about to learn; aside from my own personal test results using it.

For me, it worked like gangbusters the first time I tried it.

I wasn't totally convinced, so I let my mother try it. She has metal screws in her knee, so I figured if it still worked for her, then there must be some legitimacy to this strange stretching technique.

I learned it from Taoist Master Xiao Hong Chi, whose book about how to heal yourself naturally, recently made the bestseller list in Taiwan.

There isn't any "magical thinking" involved in this method.

It doesn't involve projecting energy or directing your intent.

But it does involve chi.

There's no visualization, special breathing or movements required.

This technique is deceptively effective.

When you're doing it, you won't believe it is working.

In fact, it can be quite uncomfortable and even painful.

This is where you must make a decision.

If you try it, be careful.

Watch the videos below and follow along precisely as instructed.

After about 5-10 minutes (if you can "hack" it) you will get up, and feel the difference almost immediately.

I cannot personally substantiate his claim of a "100% success rate" in treating thousands of diseases, but I know from personal experience this technique is by far the most effective I've tested for reducing or even eliminating physical pains and discomfort.

You can watch the introduction video here:

https://www.youtube.com/watch?v=-SAikultRIA

After that, watch these two videos to witness the technique in action during a workshop environment:

Part 1:

https://www.youtube.com/watch?v=sAGp6DuyHmg

Part 2:

https://www.youtube.com/watch?v=6Se3TopoAqc

Once you learn the technique (you can learn it in one minute) you can practice it every day for 10 minutes on each leg, and reduce, eliminate or prevent just about any malady, illness, pain or disease.

Master Hong Chi calls both the stretching technique and the "slapping method" (ouch) the Antivirus System for the whole body.

He says the "heating up" you feel is the yang chi creating the healing heat, which can be used for healing virtually any disease imaginable.

If you want scientific validation of chi, look no further than this video:

https://www.youtube.com/watch?v=vkfvv9lEXPM

You'll witness a few different demonstrations that clearly defy the laws of physics… at least our mainstream scientific understanding of them.

Master Zhou is another Qigong Master practitioner who utilizes "fire chi gong" to perform feats that would leave any magician speechless.

Even the Oprah Network has caught on to the craze.

Here's an episode of "Remedy Me!" that demonstrates an energetic process known as "Bio-Energy Healing" where an eczema sufferer receives a profound experience from healer Michael D'Alton. Bio-Energy Healing has been featured on 'First Talk', 'Joy TV', 'BCIT Magazine', 'Shaw TV', as well as the Oprah Network and W. Network:

https://www.youtube.com/watch?v=uGAAYt8_AEw

As described on his official web site www.daltonsbio.com, Michael D'Alton's Bio-Energy Healing is a gentle, yet powerful healing modality.

His form of treatment is "totally natural with no medications, needles or machines involved. It requires very little touch and is fully safe to use on all conditions. Bio-Energy Healing can be very relaxing and enjoyable to receive; a real treat for your body, mind and spirit."

Here is a wonderful demonstration video of Bio-Energy Healing:

https://www.youtube.com/watch?v=Mf-XOGZhX7w

You'll notice the similarities between Michael's "Bio-Energy" Healing and the Eastern yin/yang chi demonstrations mentioned earlier.

I encourage you to do your own in-depth research into the mysterious powers of chi. But don't just research. That won't get you anywhere.

Knowledge is useless without application, and practice.

Always keep a record of your results.

This will accelerate your progress, by providing feedback on a consistent basis, which you can use to measure your skillset as you improve through daily cultivation over a period of time.

Anything you practice gets better.

It doesn't take years of cultivating chi to use it and benefit from it.

xwAs you learned in this Mind Hack, you can experience its healing effects within as little as 5-10 minutes, even if you've never used it before.

7

MIND
HACK

How to Hack
Your Mind for
Effortless Success

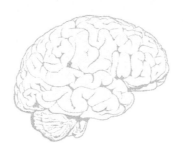

You're probably aware of the fact that certain breakthroughs, revelations and "mind tools" in the field of personal development and neurology have literally transformed our human potential.

This Mind Hack introduces a new tool you can use to greatly accelerate your progress, by subtly changing your behavior.

Most of us are 'hardwired' in a certain way, through past experiences, memories, belief structures, etc. and no matter how hard we try, our subconscious self-imposed limits and barriers leave us "stuck."

We usually end up procrastinating through a deep-seated fear of failure or rejection, and end up self-sabotaging our best efforts.

But what if there was a way out?

Imagine being able to crank your mind into high gear, magnetize financial success, hit personal goals with laser-targeted precision and wipe out any negative habits or behaviors in a matter of minutes, both painlessly and effortlessly...

Without the need for will power, self-discipline or external motivation.

Finally, technology has caught up to the latest discoveries in peak potential. It sounds incredible, but using this tool you can almost immediately begin noticing behavioral changes like:

- Your normal decision-making process suddenly changes

- You gain knowledge of things you didn't even pay attention to

- You start doing things differently than you've done them before

This can hardwire your brain for success using a powerful, but safe neural re-patterning technology. It's scientifically proven and early adopters are reporting some truly mystifying results.

Profound experiences.

Instant life changes.

You "push a button" and experience a groundbreaking advancement in audio technology for personal development... within minutes.

This isn't like binaural beats or isochronic tones.

Instead, it plugs your brain into a powerful but safe neural re-patterning technology that creates positive, profound changes in the structure of your nervous system.

This grants you the ability to rewire your brain using a 3-point neuro-imprinting process that creates changes in your brain naturally.*

*Source: www.superaffiliateninjasecrets.com/jmblog/successmovies

You'll simply find yourself doing things that make you more successful.

You'll begin to entertain more positive thoughts and emotions... you'll activate your inner-wealth magnet and attract success more easily. As stated on the official web site:

"In plain English, this amazing technology allows you to instantly transform your mental state, and enjoy the benefits of tapping into... utilizing at will a deeper level of influence, power and connection... that most folks will only touch on by accident!"

There are an unlimited number of ways to hack your brain.

These have been just a few of them I've experimented with personally, and have found positive results by practicing them regularly.

For over a decade, I've been keeping "cheat sheet" type notes on various techniques that I've tried personally, that has proven to give a positive result when applied.

You can think of the next section as your own personal Mind Hack Recipe Rolodex.

There's a magician inside all of us.

We're all connected to the same source—at the level of information.

And at this level, data can be manipulated, erased and reprogrammed with new information.

You are a super bio-computer in human form.

There is no problem you can't solve... no obstacle you can't overcome... there is nothing in your reality that can stand in your way when you learn to utilize the power of your mind to achieve laser-focus of your intent... clear out all subconscious blockages and limitations... and create anything you want to create in this life!

The
MIND
HACK
Recipe Rolodex

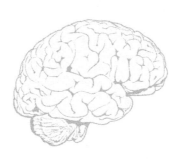

I wanted to give you direct access to the exact same techniques I've practiced and experimented with over the years, so you can benefit... use them and practice them daily yourself for amazing results!

I call this first one, "The Secret Solar Technique for Power."

It's a really cool technique you can use in the morning, to infuse a little magic into your day...

This technique uses the power of "The Sun" as a type of energetic-amplifier for the body and mind.

No, you don't need to believe that you are actually drawing energy from the Sun for this to work.

In fact, the sun you think you are seeing in the sky such a long distance away, isn't actually "out there." So your mental focus on the sun is enough to get a physical reaction from your brain, chemically.

Your mental and psychological associations to the sun are all you need to make this work.

First thing in the morning, just as the sun is rising, is the most effective time to do the following...

1. As you are waking up, move to a window where you can see the sun rising, or if you cannot see it, imagine you are in front of a window watching the majestic sun illuminate the Earth.

2. As the sun continues to rise, breathe naturally and begin to notice the warmth of the sun on your face and skin. As you begin to feel the warmth, breathe in the warming, radiating, invigorating energy.

3. Infuse imagination with tactile awareness. As you are imagining breathing in the sun's powerful energy on every inhale, it grows stronger and radiates through the entire body on every

exhale. Bask within this cycle and feel every cell of your being imbued with increasing warmth, charge and power.

4. When you feel you are "full" of this energizing force, hold your breath for just a few moments while feeling the radiant sun's energy glowing inside...

5. Then let go and exhale while allowing the sunlight within to expand outward in all directions, with the intention of creating a miracle today... something unexpected, yet appreciated. Something amazing. Don't limit the manifestation; let it be free.

Your higher intelligence knows exactly what to "do" with this new radiant energy.

Your only job is to do the technique, feel the effects, intend for a miracle utilizing this powerful solar energy, and then completely LET GO.

Then, just go about your day as usual.

After trying this technique for a few days, let me know of any miracles or unexpected blessings that "magically" come your way.

Here are a few more bonus "Mind Hack" Recipes for your experimentation…

To Balance a Negative Condition

Put your feet apart but keep them equally-spaced on the floor. Sit up straight and let your hands drop into your lap, or on your knees without touching each other.

Hold the index, middle finger and thumb of each hand in a sort of triangle composed of the first two fingers and the thumb.

Once you're feeling relaxed, take a deep breath and hold it for a count of seven—then slowly release it. Take a short rest, then repeat again taking another deep breath and holding it until you've done this seven times. After this, change your position completely and put it out of your mind.

This alone is normally enough to counter-balance most negative conditions. But in some cases such as deep-seated or chronic stress, the technique should be repeated until one has a positive result.

It usually takes about two hours before the results start to appear, so be patient with this technique.

The quicker you perform this technique for yourself as soon as you feel yourself falling out of balance, the easier you can generally normalize the condition, tension or stress.

To Balance an Over-Positive Condition

As in the previous technique, get comfortable and put your feet equally on the floor but this time let your feet touch each other.

Your fingers should also be touching. Hold them at chest level in front of you, with your thumbs touching and each finger touching the tip of its corresponding finger on the opposite hand. Now slowly and gently close your eyes, and take a deep breath inward.

Let out the breath while counting to the number six, and once again feel yourself becoming completely relaxed. Exhale slowly for about five or six breaths until you feel totally relaxed. Then repeat, holding the breath for a count of five.

Repeat this technique five times, and then stop. Resume breathing at your regular pace and simply put the technique out of your mind completely.

This is called a "negative balancing" technique to bring balance and alignment where there exists excess positive energy (think of the positive and negative charge of a battery). This technique has been secretly used for ages to reverse such conditions as the common cold. The symptoms of a cold are the outer-evidence of the body's attempt to clear itself of invasion by various micro-organisms.

A "positive" balancing technique simply isn't effective in these types of circumstances but the "negative" balancing charge will usually assist the internal system in greatly decreasing or eliminating the invaders within about six to eight hours or less.

To Vastly Improve Your Memory

1. When arriving in any new area for the first time, close your eyes for a moment and see how many objects in the room you can name—pictures, chairs, desks, tables, anything you can recall. Do this every time you enter any place that's new to you.

2. After going up or down a flight of steps mentally recount how many steps were there.

3. In the evening, recall the first thing you did when you left the house this morning—or, if you didn't go anywhere, what did you do? Try to recall about three to four minutes of this, but no more.

Tomorrow, recall what you did in any other 3-minute interval of your day.

Practice these techniques for about two or three weeks, and you'll begin to grasp the real purpose of these exercises and might even design some similar techniques of your own.

Don't let the simplicity of these fool you; they aren't to be underestimated. No true mental control can be developed without the essential fundamental skills gained from this type of self-development.

To Greatly Enhance Your Power of Concentration

1. Take any two numbers of two digits each (i.e. "36" and "29") mentally—without using a calculator or a piece of paper. Practice and check your answers afterward. Do this until you're positive you have the correct answer in your head, before you verify the results.

2. Go look up any poem or song lyrics—regardless of length—and commit four lines at a time to your memory. Practice them until you know them by heart. Then, memorize four more lines in

addition to the previous. Continue doing this until you have memorized the entire poem or song.

Increase your memory skills by memorizing the first four sentences of a book. Then, memorize four more sentences. Only practice these memorization techniques once per day. After just a few weeks of this simple daily practice, your memory skills will begin to astonish you.

3. The next time you pass someone one the street or anywhere else where you can see the person for a small amount of time before they vanish into the distance, choose the person and look very closely into their eyes. Once they've passed out of your field of vision, hold the picture of the person's face in mind, and contemplate their expression. Feel what they're feeling. Sense their essence.

You might soon realize this technique is designed to take you far above and beyond what you currently think you understand about feeling energy, essence and bio-energetic vibrations.

Routine practice of this technique can be quite a rewarding experience.

With no additional effort after some time, you might discover that you're beginning to develop a capacity for tuning into the people whose faces and expressions you're holding in front of you!

You might even become aware of their dominant emotional sensations. Oftentimes you'll sense fear because in these days so many individuals are saturating themselves in fear, more so than just about any other emotion. People in general are more likely to respond to the fear of loss than the prospect of gaining something. This is known as a golden rule in marketing, advertising and business.

Once you practice and increase your sensitivity to these subtle sensations, you may find yourself tuning into the very thought-forms of the person you're focusing your attention upon.

When you put your brain to work like this, you can observe it working.

By these observations of your brain activity, you'll gradually begin to increase the information capacity by which you can observe, retain and recall information at will... even to the point of reading into the thoughts and emotions others are processing!

To Project a Thought into Action

1.   Choose a specific location where you'll be free from being interrupted for at least five minutes.

     Sit down in an upright chair with your feet touching each other but do not cross them.

     Let your hands rest easily in your lap and relax keeping your back straight and your spine in alignment. Just become aware of yourself breathing naturally. Close your eyes and imagine the color blue. (The shade of blue doesn't matter, simply choose one shade of blue for the meditation.)

     See the color of blue all around you, filling the space of the room you are in. Stay focused but don't think about "trying" to do this too much—just imagine the entire area is saturated in this color.

Do this for one full minute.

When time's up, spend another minute imagining any shade of pink, and then yet another minute imagining the purest white—the color of new-fallen snowflakes in the sun. Don't spend any longer than three minutes in total. Once you're done, take a deep breath and relax. Then proceed...

2. Think of a sound, like a violin playing in the background. It can be any tune that comes to mind. But it has to be the sound of a violin playing the tune. If other instruments begin to appear, separate out just the sound of the violin until all you can hear is the one instrument playing the tune.

Do this for just one minute.

For the next minute afterward, hear the sound of a horn playing the same tune. Only the one instrument is allowed to be heard at a time. Focus only on this one instrument as it plays.

For the final minute, imagine a piano playing the same tune. Just the piano and no other instrument. This can be a little more difficult because in lieu of single notes, there are entire chords and complex combinations of those chords mixed in with the melody.

Just imagine it—nothing more.

After the third minute, once again breathe deeply and relax.

3. This is a different type of technique. In the first two you were hearing sounds and seeing colors and you were leveraging your will power to block out all other sights, sounds and colors. But in this technique, you'll utilize your will power differently.

As before, go through the simple relaxation process (which should be second nature by now) and once your eyes are closed, see the color pink engulfing your entire body and saturating the space around you completely. But this time see a LIGHT pink color, like as in a ray of la-ser-light.

Don't just see this in front and to both sides of you, but literally all around and through you.

Envelop yourself completely in this pink cloud and let it extend six to ten inches outward in all directions. Hold onto this mental image for one minute and then put it out of your mind. Relax.

To Gain Control of Your Emotions

1.   Go find a box of regular matches. Open the box and turn it upside down, causing the matches to spill across the table. Mix them all around, and then slowly and consciously place them all back in the box one-by-one, with each of the match tips pointing upward in

the same direction. If you think this technique is pointless, guess again. This is great for cultivating emotional stability. Very simple.

2. Turn on your television at regular volume but don't face the screen. Turning your head in the opposite direction, attempt to hear and understand everything that is being done and said. Imagine the visual images corresponding to the sounds you're hearing.

Do this simple technique once per day until you feel you've mastered it. At first, you may not realize the emotional training involved in this technique but keep doing it and you'll fully understand.

3. This third and final technique you can do daily, any place, at absolutely any time. It's quite different from the previous two techniques; it involves how you relate to others...

Here's the technique:

Slow down... **and observe.**

When you're walking, let someone pass ahead of you and just observe this process slowly. If you're driving, slow it down to slightly less than the legal speed limit.

When you see another car coming up behind you, let them pass. And observe.

Not just how you are feeling as you do this, but observe the totality of the entire process at large.

Every time you enter or leave a room, allow anyone near you to go first. Each time, carry a bright smile on your face and in your eyes. And observe every process and interaction that follows.

I guarantee if you practice this technique for 30 days straight, you'll become an entirely new person.

To Understand Cause and Effect

1. "For every action, there is an equal, and op-
    posite reaction" as Einstein so eloquently put
    it. Take nothing for granted. Everything has a
    cause… and every cause has an effect. You
    can call this "Karma" or "Yin/Yang" or "Judg-
    ment" or anything else you prefer. The simple
    truth remains…

For every cause, there is an effect. And for every effect, there is causation.

You can begin to contemplate basic relationships, like
putting your finger too close to a flame will cause you to
feel pain from a burning finger. Or dropping a dry towel
into a pale of water will cause it to come out soaked.

After awhile, contemplate more subtle relationships
such as the cause of a violent protest or rally.

You might discover upon your meditation that perhaps a prolonged heat-spell along with feelings of injustice coupled with social status and "the need to fit in" are all contributing connections to the causation of violence. Perhaps they've been malnourished and these things only serve to create even stronger tension and emotional disharmony.

Maybe some of them were paid money to initiate violence within the protest. Yes, this happens.

Attempt to analyze four news stories or incidents per day. You won't always be completely accurate, but the more you train your brain to work in these new ways, the more information you will begin to receive that seemingly defies any other logical explanation.

You are strengthening your sixth sense by incorporating these techniques into your daily practice.

To Store More Energy in Only 2 ½ Minutes

1. Sit up straight but don't tense any part of your body. Keep your weight evenly balanced between both of your feet.

2. Breathe in deeply, and count to five.

3. Feel yourself relax and breathe out for the count of ten.

4. Rinse and repeat.

5. While doing this technique, close your mouth firmly and press your jaws in tight, while clenching both hands into a fist. As you're breathing in and out, imagine that each and every breath is bringing with it a SURGE of positive energy and raw power that you are storing inside of you.

To feel an even stronger effect, as you are breathing this powerful energy inward with each inhale, send the energetic force down into the pit of your stomach just around the belly button area, and feel it being held there. This area is called the "dan tien" and is a literal storehouse for energy.

After doing this technique for about 15 to 20 minutes, you'll feel a very noticeable vibration in the area which you are storing the energy repeatedly. This exhilarating energy will supercharge your body and being for the next several hours!

Gradually you'll increase the capacity for your energetic storehouse and within 30 days or less, you might find that you become somewhat impervious to most ailments, illness and diseases.

A Technique for Reversing Illness

1. Sit up comfortably, but with your head and spine erect. Move your feet an equal distance apart and rest your hands loosely in your lap.

2. Surround yourself (in your imagination) with a very bright, white cloud of light. Feel it envelop your body and being from the inside-out.

3. Now concentrate that white light in the area of illness within the body. Increase this concentration and feel its corresponding effects as you mentally increase the tension and vibration focused in this one area of illness within the body.

4. For example, if you're having some trouble in the heart or in the lungs, imagine the concentration of the white light in the fifth and seventh thoracic vertebrae of the spine, just between and slightly below your shoulder blades.

Most of your automatic bodily functions are controlled and maintained by the sympathetic nervous system. Focusing additional energy into the appropriate points of the sympathetic nervous system parallel to the spine stimulates the natural healing processes and speeds up normalization of the affected area of the body.

5. If you're experiencing a nervous disorder, you can concentrate the white light in the area of the fifth cervical vertebrae to bring almost instantaneous relief and make the nervous system stronger.

To Bring Relief to a Headache

1. This one is especially effective. You can often find complete relief of a headache by placing the tips of both of your first two fingers of your right hand onto your left temple, while placing the index and middle fingers of the left hand softly against the right temple.

2. Next you'll envision a flow of "psychic" energy (in however way you wish) going from the fingers of your right hand into the left temple, then out the right temple into the fingers of the left hand. After only three to four minutes, you might notice the headache suddenly vanishes!

If it returns, then there is causation. Repeat the technique every time a headache is experienced and as you're doing it, pay close attention to any thoughts, ideas, memories or emotions that occur.

As always, the more you practice the technique, the faster and easier it works.

To Send Divine "Healing" Energy to Someone

1. Namaste literally means, "The divine essence within me, acknowledges the divine essence within you." By this simple act of infinite com-passion, love and kindness—by recognizing and acknowledging the divine nature within another person that is the same divine nature within you—this begins to create a warm feeling of self-love and love for others... love for creation... adoration and gratitude... these majestic higher vibrations can be imagined as a bright-pink, glowing aura which projects from the field of the heart and completely engulfs the entire body.

2. When you can feel these higher vibrations around and inside you, bring your mental attention to the person, place or group that you wish to broadcast this infinite divine "healing" energy to.

3. Using your will power forcefully broadcast your bright-pink engulfed auric field imbued with pure divine essence into the person, place or object of your intent. Allow the natural sensations of bliss, love and unity engulf the subject, infusing this divinity into their own. Feel the entanglement as you breathe in and out, growing and glowing with this loving but powerful, bright-pink cloud of light.

4. The mission has been accomplished. Put it completely out of your mind and relax.

To Extract Higher Vibrations of Psychic Energy from the Air

1. To extract "chi", "ki", "life force", "prana" or "psychic" energetic vibrations from the air, go find an open window or stand in an area outdoors where you can breathe in some fresh air.

2. Put your feet apart and outstretch your arms horizontally, pointing straight outward.

3. Breathe in slowly, inhaling to a count of five.

4. Now exhale, emptying your lungs to the count of ten. Counting on the inhale and the exhale should be at the same pace.

5. Repeat this breathing technique ten times in a row.

You will soon begin strongly feeling these higher vibrations of psychic energy. Use this wisely.

I sincerely hope you've enjoyed these mind hacks and I look forward to sharing more with you in the very near future. If you're not one of my subscribers yet, subscribe and be kept informed on the latest research and experiments in consciousness technology on my Self Development Blog at:

www.personaldevelopmentwithjason.com/blog

Enjoy.

ABOUT THE AUTHOR
JASON MANGRUM

Jason Mangrum is a best-selling author, a personal development consultant, a marketing strategist, success coach and visionary who has helped thousands of people from around the world access greater potential for wealth, better health and happiness for over 15 years.

His unique approach to energetic science and studies of the mind and consciousness have unlocked dormant abilities long-forgotten that are readily available for anyone to access, once they know the secrets.

You can get more information on his book Uberman at:

www.personaldevelopmentwithjason.com/get-uberman

Connect with him on Facebook to inquire about his personal consultation services and "Quantum Entanglement Sessions" at:

www.facebook.com/themindofpower

Or send a personal email to:

beyondsuperhuman@gmail.com
Subject: "Quantum Entanglement Sessions"

He utilizes a unique, intuitive and energetic process for connecting remotely to 'entangle' the energy field of the problem or issue with a higher state of awareness, quickly resulting in noticeable changes, even from a distance.

Clients often report instant and profound results from the sessions.

To subscribe to his Personal Development Blog and stay up to date with his latest research, visit:

www.personaldevelopmentwithjason.com/blog

Other Products & Solutions for Self-Development

Uberman: Almost Super Human: The original bestseller for Self-Empowerment, Manifestation, Consciousness Exploration, Self-Healing and much more. (Amazon retailers are selling physical copies of this book for up to $1,000!)

www.personaldevelopmentwithjason.com/get-uberman

Super Affiliate Ninja Secrets: An important part of Self Development is improving your finances. A book about a simple ninja method being used to win affiliate competitions with no web site, no list and without using any of your own products. (Includes step-by-step screen shots)

www.superaffiliateninjasecrets.com

Morgan James
Speakers Group

↗ www.TheMorganJamesSpeakersGroup.com

We connect Morgan James published
authors with live and online events
and audiences whom will benefit
from their expertise.

Morgan James makes all of our titles available
through the Library for All Charity Organization.

www.LibraryForAll.org

Printed in the USA
CPSIA information can be obtained
at www.ICGtesting.com
JSHW082356140824
68134JS00020B/2106

9 781683 502524